Mammals on the Move

BY: MELISSA WHITTINGTON

Lion

The king of the jungle, lions live in prides with social hierarchies and impressive roars.

Elephant

The largest land mammal, elephants are highly intelligent with strong family bonds and trunks for grabbing and trumpeting.

Zebras

Known for their black and white stripes, zebras live in herds and are surprisingly fast runners.

Giraffe

The tallest land mammal, giraffes have long necks for reaching high leaves and excellent eyesight.

Chimpanzee

Our closest living relative, chimpanzees are highly intelligent with complex social behaviors and use tools.

Gorilla

The largest primate, gorillas are peaceful herbivores living in family groups and known for their impressive strength.

Orangutan

Found in rainforests, orangutans are intelligent apes known for their climbing skills and reddish fur.

Dolphins

Playful and social, dolphins are marine mammals known for their intelligence, acrobatics, and clicks and whistles.

Whale

The largest animal on Earth, whales are gentle giants with complex songs and baleen plates for filtering food.

Bear

Powerful omnivores, bears come in various species like grizzly bears with powerful claws and polar bears adapted for arctic life.

Kangaroo

Found in Australia, kangaroos are hopping marsupials with pouches for carrying young and strong kicks.

Koala

Adorable marsupials with grey fur, koalas spend most of their time in eucalyptus trees eating leaves.

Lemur

lemurs come from Madagascar and have large eyes and a long, bushy tail.

Deer

Graceful herbivores, deer come in various types with impressive antlers for males and excellent hearing and leaping ability.

Wolf

Social predators, wolves live in packs and play a vital role in ecosystems by controlling prey populations.

Fox

Cunning and adaptable, foxes are smaller predators with keen senses and known for their bushy tails.

Rabbit

Cute and quick, rabbits are burrowing herbivores with strong digging claws and long ears for hearing predators.

Bat

The only flying mammal, bats navigate using echolocation and are vital pollinators for many plants.

Hippopotamus

Semi-aquatic herbivores, hippopotamuses spend most of their time in water and have large tusks and powerful bites.

Good Bye!